I0789239

Easy Sudoku Puzzles

Easy Sudoku Puzzles 1

Sudoku Puzzle 1

1	4	2		9				5
7			4				8	9
8		5					2	4
2					4	8		
	3				1	2	6	
	8			7	2	9	4	1
	5		2		6			
	2	8			9	4	1	
	7	9	1		8	5	3	

Sudoku Puzzle 2

1				9	4	7		5
5	7	3	1		2			
	4			5	3	1		8
	8	1	5	6	7	3	4	
			8		1			7
	5	6	4		9			2
4	6						9	
	3		9	1			7	6
9				4				

Easy Sudoku Puzzles 2

Sudoku Puzzle 1

	8					7	9	3
	1		9	8	5			
	6			7			1	
	4		7	2		3	6	
3	5		8			1	7	
		7	3		1		8	
1			4	6	7	8		9
5	9			3			2	
	7		5			6	3	1

Sudoku Puzzle 2

6				5		7	2	3
7			1	2	6			9
2		5		4	3			6
	6	1	2		4		7	5
	2	7				3	9	4
				8	7	2		
	7	6						
1			8			6	5	7
9	3			7	5			

Easy Sudoku Puzzles 3

Sudoku Puzzle 1

		6	9	2	3			
		2		6	1	3	4	5
	1		4		5	2		6
	3						8	
7	4		5		6			
								9
	6		8		4		7	2
2	8	9	6		7	4		1
	7	4	2		9		6	8

Sudoku Puzzle 2

8	2	5						6
			9		3	2	7	8
			8	2	6	1	5	
			2	6				
	8	9	5	1		4	2	
7		2			4		6	5
	5		4			6		
2		6			8	5	3	7
				3	5		4	2

Easy Sudoku Puzzles 4

Sudoku Puzzle 1

6	7	9	3					
4			7	9	2			6
	1		5	8	6		4	
		8						
		3	1	6	8	2	9	7
2		7		5	9	3		
						9		
8	5		9	2	1			
9	3			4	7	5	8	2

Sudoku Puzzle 2

	2	4						7
7	6					8	2	
8	9		7	4				
5	8				6			
			5	9		6	4	
9			2	7	8	1	5	
4		9				7	6	5
3			1	6	7		9	2
6	7	2			4		8	

Easy Sudoku Puzzles 5

Sudoku Puzzle 1

8	1				5	4		
		7	9					6
2	6		7	8			9	1
	4		3			6		2
9		6					1	5
3	2		6	7	1			8
		2			8	7	5	
7		3	4	2		1	8	
4			5			2		

Sudoku Puzzle 2

	8		5				1	7
1					8		5	9
9		5				6	3	
4	6	3	8	7	9	1		5
8		2					4	
		7		2	4		8	
7	5	9	2	8				4
		8	7	3				1
6						8		2

Easy Sudoku Puzzles 6

Sudoku Puzzle 1

			3		9	4	8	1
4	2	9	1		5			7
	1	8		4		5		
	4		9				5	
9	3	5	4			2		
	7	2	5	3	8		1	
7			8	1			2	
		3				8		6
		4	6	5	3			

Sudoku Puzzle 2

			2	9		5		
					5	7		2
2		9	3		7	8		4
	2		7	5	3	9		
4	7		9					
	9	5	4	2	6		3	
				7	2		5	1
5		4			9			6
7	6	2	5		1		8	

Easy Sudoku Puzzles 7

Sudoku Puzzle 1

9			2		8	6	4	
	8	3	5					2
4			7	3		1	8	5
	1	5		7	6		9	
	6	9	4		3			8
8			9		1			
			6	9	7		2	1
7			3			5		9
6				4			3	

Sudoku Puzzle 2

7		3	9	8			5	1
			1	7		3	8	6
8	1				3	7	2	9
		2	4	3	6	8		
6	4	5						
9				5				7
2	9	7				5		
4			7		9			8
		1	6	4		9		

Easy Sudoku Puzzles 8

Sudoku Puzzle 1

					6	7		
1	2			8			4	5
4	7			3				9
7	8	9	1	2	3			
3		2		6	5	1	9	7
		1		9	4	8	3	2
5						9	7	
	1	7			8	4		
		8		7		3		

Sudoku Puzzle 2

2	7			4	1			8
		8	3		5		1	
		3		2		7	4	
6	3		8			5	7	
9			1			6		
1	2			3		8		4
7		1		8	3		6	
8		9		6	7	1		2
3						4	8	

Easy Sudoku Puzzles 9

Sudoku Puzzle 1

	7	4	9		2	5	3	
	6	2	8					4
	8		4	1	7	9	6	2
		7		2				6
4	5				9	2		
	2				6		5	1
	3			5			4	9
		5	2		3	8		7
	9				4			5

Sudoku Puzzle 2

	5		4	3				
1		4	8	6				2
	3						4	8
4		2		5	8			
5			3	9		4	8	6
6		3			4	2		5
	6		7	2	1			
7	2	9		4	3			
	4		9	8		5		7

Easy Sudoku Puzzles 10

Sudoku Puzzle 1

3	9						4	6
			9	3	7	2		8
	7			6				5
	1	3		2		8	6	
2				9	3	1		7
				1	8	4		2
8							2	1
	3			5			7	4
5		4	1	7		9	8	3

Sudoku Puzzle 2

	9	8	7		2		3	6
		5	6	9	8			
2		4	1				7	
8	4		5			6		3
9			4					8
	7	6					1	4
				1	3		6	5
3	1	2			6	4		
	5		8	7		3	2	

Medium Sudoku Puzzles 1

Medium Sudoku Puzzles 1

Sudoku Puzzle 1

		1				9	4	
4		7	8	3		2	1	
9		6	5			8		3
8			6					
				2		1	3	
					3	5		
5	7				2	4	8	
1	6			9			5	
			4	1				7

Sudoku Puzzle 2

	7	4			9	5		
1				7		8	3	4
3		2			4			1
		1	9	4		6	7	5
	8	6	3	1				
		7	5					3
	2			6	3			
			2		5			
	9					4		

Medium Sudoku Puzzles 2

Sudoku Puzzle 1

3	9		4		6			
		7				3		2
		6	3	7		5		
		3		4	9			
7	6					4	5	
9		4		6	7		1	
1	5			3			2	6
4								
		9			2		4	7

Sudoku Puzzle 2

	8	3			2			
		9	4			6		
5			9			3		
1			8				3	2
6		2		3	4			
4			5	2			6	7
3	7	1	2					
9	2					7		4
8			1	6				

Medium Sudoku Puzzles 3

Sudoku Puzzle 1

			1	7			8	
3		5			8		6	
8	1							
9	7			8		6	1	
	5					9		
6	4			9	3		5	
	6	4	9			7		8
7	8	9	5		2			
			8	4				

Sudoku Puzzle 2

	7			6				3
	9	4	7					
8		6		4	2	5		
			3	9				
4	1		5	7	6	3	2	8
							1	9
3			4			6		
		7	1	5	8			4
					9	1		

Medium Sudoku Puzzles 4

Sudoku Puzzle 1

8		1		5			7	
7					6			
		4		2		8		
		7	8		2		4	
4				9		1	6	3
5		6	1					
6							5	
2	3			7	4		1	8
	7		9		5	4		

Sudoku Puzzle 2

					4		9	
		7						8
		3						6
	1		8	2		7		
5						3		2
4		2		7	6			1
7	2	4		3		8	1	5
9	6			1			4	3
				5	2	6		

Medium Sudoku Puzzles 5

Sudoku Puzzle 1

3	9			1	7			
7		4						2
2				5		9	7	
	7	9			2	8	3	1
5						6		
		6	8		4			
8		2			3	7		
	1			9	8	5		
		7					8	6

Sudoku Puzzle 2

3	9	1	8		4			
	5							9
				5	9			8
		4				7		
		3					1	
9		5		3	2		6	4
8				6	3	5		2
			2	4			7	
4	3		7	1	5			

Medium Sudoku Puzzles 6

Sudoku Puzzle 1

2	6	1					4	9
7			3	1	2		6	
	3			6			1	7
1		3	5			6	8	
		9						
			8			9		1
			2				7	
				4	9	5		2
3	5	2	1					

Sudoku Puzzle 2

5	9							3
	6	4		8				
7	8	2		5			9	
	2		5	7		4		
	5							2
9	7	6	4					
					3	9	2	5
2	1					8	3	
		5	2	6	9			

Medium Sudoku Puzzles 7

Sudoku Puzzle 1

			8		7			
	1		4			9	7	3
				3		5	8	
		2						
			5		6	1	4	
6	4	7		1	8	3		
	6	8	1	5		2		7
	9		3			8		
			7			4		6

Sudoku Puzzle 2

	8	1						
	9	7		8	1			
		6	7	9	3	1		4
9		5	6	2				
6	4		1			8		
					5	7	9	6
	2		8					
	6	9					3	8
5					4			2

Medium Sudoku Puzzles 8

Sudoku Puzzle 1

	7		8	5	2	9		3
	4			3	6			
3			7			1		
			9	6			1	4
8		7						5
				2			8	
4		2		7		8		1
	1		2	4		6		7
			3				9	

Sudoku Puzzle 2

	3		5	1				
1						3		
	9				7		1	5
5		6	2			9		7
8		3	9	6		5	2	
								4
6		7	8	4		1		
	2	4						8
		1	3			6	4	

Medium Sudoku Puzzles 9

Sudoku Puzzle 1

5	4						9	2
		8	5	1	9			
			4		2		6	5
7	2			8				9
						4	5	
				9	4			
		5				9		6
	8	6		2	3			7
1		2	6		7	3		

Sudoku Puzzle 2

	4					3		7
8	6	7	1	3	2	5	9	
	3						2	8
			5				8	
					7	6		
		5		8		9	4	
			8	7			5	6
7		3	6					
2	5			1				3

Medium Sudoku Puzzles 10

Sudoku Puzzle 1

		5			8	6		1
7				2				9
8	4						3	
	7	3	6	8	5	1		
	5		2					
2	9			1				3
		7			2	8	5	4
6							1	7
			7	9			2	

Sudoku Puzzle 2

			1	2				
5				6			8	3
7			4			6		9
8					1		6	
4	9		8					
					3		9	2
		6	5		2			
2	1			8	9	4	5	6
	5			1			3	7

Hard Sudoku Puzzles 1

Hard Sudoku Puzzles 1

Sudoku Puzzle 1

2		8			7	3		
	4		8					
	7					9	6	
	6	5						
	3	1				6		5
	2	9	6				7	
6	9						2	1
				5	1			6

Sudoku Puzzle 2

					9			
1	5			3		7		4
	9		1		8			
9								5
		5		1	3			7
8		6						
4	2	3					8	
	1	7		5				
5						1		

Hard Sudoku Puzzles 2

Sudoku Puzzle 1

					3	5		
9	8	3		1			7	
		6				4	8	
3				7				2
5							9	1
4				6				8
		2		5				
					6	9		7
			4		8			

Sudoku Puzzle 2

5						8		
8				1		4		6
				2				
1						6		
	2		3	8				9
9	6					5	7	
					5			
		6	8		7		1	4
	1		4					8

Hard Sudoku Puzzles 3

Sudoku Puzzle 1

								6
1							8	9
	2	4	3					
	4		8			7		1
6					2	5		
9	1							
		1			9			
	9	8			3	4	1	
		2		7	1			

Sudoku Puzzle 2

8	5							3
	1	4			3	7		8
				8	2			
9		1	6	4	5			7
							5	
							9	2
5		6						
2	9	3						
				7		6		

Hard Sudoku Puzzles 4

Sudoku Puzzle 1

						9		
	2		6	4		8	5	
					1		3	
				1		6		
		8	5	3				
	6	3		7	2			5
								8
3			7	9		5	4	
							1	6

Sudoku Puzzle 2

9					6	4	7	
2	1				5			
6								5
		7	3			9		
4		5	6	8	1		2	3
				9				
	3							1
		6	9	7				
				4				

Hard Sudoku Puzzles 5

Sudoku Puzzle 1

7					9			
2		8		3		7		4
6								
				9	7		6	
9	1							
5	4				2			
		3		1			9	
						3	7	
1	2			4	3		8	

Sudoku Puzzle 2

	4			8			9	
			3				1	6
	5		1			2		
	1		9	6	4		5	
		6						9
3						1		
	8			3	5	9		
								2
7		9						3

Hard Sudoku Puzzles 6

Sudoku Puzzle 1

	3	5					7	1
			8					4
			3					9
				5	4			
3	9					2		
7		6			9			
1		7		6		4		
			5		2	7		
	6					3	9	

Sudoku Puzzle 2

3			9	7		5		
	4					1	9	
2						3	6	7
6					9			
						2		
		1	4					
	6		7	3	8			5
7	9	8	5				4	

Hard Sudoku Puzzles 7

Sudoku Puzzle 1

8				1	6		4	
		4				2		
				3	2	9		
1		5						
	3	6		7	8	4	9	1
			2					3
3	9	2						
4					7	5		

Sudoku Puzzle 2

9							8	
3			7					4
	6			2	3			
						6	7	
		3	4					9
		7						1
7					5	9	6	
	1	5	8		9			
8			3				2	

Hard Sudoku Puzzles 8

Sudoku Puzzle 1

	6			8			1	
	9			7			6	
2	1						8	
	7	6	9		5			
	5							9
			1			5	3	4
1			3					
8							9	
	3			5				7

Sudoku Puzzle 2

				6	2	4		
		8						9
						3		
8			9			7		5
			3	5				8
	5		6			2		
7		9	8			1		
		3						
			7	4		5	2	3

Hard Sudoku Puzzles 9

Sudoku Puzzle 1

5		9	4					
		7				6	5	
			1					
	9			6			3	
	3		5			7	4	1
	7				1			2
				7	4	3		
	4	2						
9	1		6					

Sudoku Puzzle 2

					2			
2	4	7						5
	1				3		8	
					4		9	1
			8			2	3	
	2	4		6				
				8				6
7	9			5	1			
4	3	8						

Hard Sudoku Puzzles 10

Sudoku Puzzle 1

	1		9					
4			5		6			
			1		7		3	8
	7	9					2	
3				6	1		5	
		8						
	8							
	4				8	1	6	9
2				4	5			

Sudoku Puzzle 2

	2		5				8	
				3	4			
				1				
4	3							9
1	9	5		6	3			
			9				6	
9	5					4	2	
	6		8					5
	4	7				1		

Sudoku

Hard Puzzle 3

					8		9	
		3			1			
2					7	6		
				2				
	9	4		8		2		
7	1			4		9		5
1			9			5	3	
5	7					8	4	
					6		2	1

Sudoku

Hard Puzzle 4

7			1			2	
			2	7			1
	2	5		8			4
		9					
6		1			9	5	3
		3			1		
							9
2		7	5				
		2	3		4	8	

Sudoku

Hard Puzzle 5

2	7						9	3
		6		3	9			
3						1	5	
	3		2		4			7
9	2	5				4		8
4			6					
							7	5
5					8			1
		4			3	9		

Sudoku

Hard Puzzle 6

8	4					7		1
				8			5	
		6						4
	7		1	3		4		
	2	3				1	9	8
			5					3
7	9							
				2				9
		8		4			3	

Sudoku

Hard Puzzle 1

								2
						9	4	
		3						5
	9	2	3		5		7	4
8	4							
	6	7		9	8			
			7		6			
			9				2	
4		8	5			3	6	

Sudoku

Hard Puzzle 2

4		6					5	9
				4		2		
	7							
		5	9	1			6	
	1	3				8	9	4
			2					1
5		8						
				3				8
	4			6		1		

Sudoku

Hard Puzzle 3

					8		9	
		3			1			
2					7	6		
				2				
	9	4		8		2		
7	1			4		9		5
1			9			5	3	
5	7					8	4	
					6		2	1

Sudoku

Hard Puzzle 4

	7			1			2	
5				2	7			1
		2	5		8			4
			9					
8	6		1			9	5	3
			3			1		
3								9
	2		7	5				
			2	3		4	8	

Sudoku

Hard Puzzle 6

8	4					7		1
				8			5	
		6						4
	7		1	3		4		
	2	3				1	9	8
			5					3
7	9							
				2				9
		8		4			3	

Sudoku #7

1	5				9			
		9						
		6	7			1	9	
	9	4				5		6
				8		3		7
	6	7			3			
9	4		8					1
				6		2	5	
			2					8

Sudoku

					8		9	
		3			1			
2					7	6		
				2				
	9	4		8		2		
7	1			4		9		5
1			9			5	3	
5	7					8	4	
					6		2	1

Sudoku #1

		1	8		3	9		
	9						1	
5				7				8
9								3
		5	4		2	7		
		8	5		7	1		
	5						4	
		9	7		5	6		
2				6				1

Sudoku #2

9	4		1					
			3			2	8	
					7			5
8	1			4			5	
							4	
6				8			2	3
					5		7	2
3		9			6			
	7		2					

Sudoku #3

9			8		5		1	
1	3			2				
	4			9				
	7				3		2	
		1		8			7	
		2		7				9
					8			6
					9	5		1
		9	1	3		4		

Sudoku #4

							1	7
6	4	5	2					
	1							
		4			8			
		2	5			6		
						5		
	8			7	1			
					3			

Sudoku #5

9		1					8	
			6		7			3
	6							
	5				3			7
							9	
			8					
			9	1				
4	2							6

Sudoku #6

			6		3			
6			5					4
							7	
				9				1
	2							
	3	7						
8						3		
							2	
1			4	5				

Sudoku #8

			8		4			
	3					5	2	
		7						
	5			2				
				9	3			8
				5			3	
		8	6					4
		9						

Sudoku #1

						3		5
1			7					
						8		
	5			3				4
6			9				7	
	6							
			1		7		9	
	8	3						

Sudoku #2

	5		9					
		8				4		
					3		2	
							6	9
		3						
		4		8	1			
	6							
7	9							
					4	1		

Sudoku #3

							4	
1		9		3				
		8		9	6			
		1	4		5			
						1		3
			2					
				8		9		
	4						5	

Sudoku #4

			8	5				
		3	6			4		7
8	2						1	
5								
					4			2
		4			7			
			2				8	
3								

Sudoku #5

		5				8		
					7			3
		6	8		4		1	
	7				1	6		
	4		6			3	9	
5	6			4		2		
		1			9			
	2							6
6				2	5			8

Sudoku #6

	5		7				6	
1	7						4	9
				9	3			
4	8						9	3
5	9			8	1		7	4
			2					
8	1			7	9		5	2
				6	5			

Sudoku #7

	2							
5		3		9		8		
9			5		2	4		
7	1			3	4	2	9	
		4				6		
8								7
1					5	3		2
3			2	4		7		
							8	

Sudoku #8

		9	5				1	
	1					2		
3				1	4			9
4			1					2
2			4					7
	9			2	7	8		
		8	7				5	
	5					6		
7				5	3			8

Sudoku #1

	2		6				1	7
5	6	3				8		2
6		9		7				
		5	4		6	2	9	
	3							
	1	2		4	5			8
8				1	2	3		

Sudoku #2

		8						
				4	3			
9		6				8		
			6		7			
							3	
	5						4	1
						6		9
	4	5		1				

Sudoku #3

			6			9		4
6			7					2
3				8				
8	7			9		6		5
				2	6		7	
		2	5	7				
9	3				4			
				1				3
4					9			6

Sudoku #4

4					2			8
		1		6	8			
2		6	7				9	
1					9			
			6					2
	6	2				8	4	
	2				5	9		1
8			2					3
			8	7		6		

Sudoku #5

4						7	6	
	3		8	9				
							2	9
6					7			
	5		4					
		9		2				8
					6			4

Sudoku #6

		4						
			2				3	
		6			9			
				5		6		4
						9		
1			3			8		
2							9	
3								
					6	7		

Sudoku #7

	7		8				6	
		3			2	5		9
					4		7	
5						7		
	1							5
		7	6				9	
		9		8				
1	8			2			3	
		6	1			2		

Sudoku #8

		7				2	1	
9			6		5			
		1		2				
3			7					
							4	5
	5				4			6
				1				7

Sudoku #1

8			4	2			9	
							6	
7	3		8	1	6			
			6	8	7		4	
9							1	3
						2		
	2					4	3	
3		8	7					9

Sudoku #2

		7			6			
		5						
			4				8	
8			1					
				2				5
4								
					4			
9	1						4	
				5	7	2		

Sudoku #3

		3		2				5
	7			4				
								9
		2						
						8	1	
9		5		6				
		6						1
			7		3	4		
					8			

Sudoku #4

							9	
	8			4	7			
								2
	4	7				5		
			2		3		1	
		9						
1		2			6			
				7		4		

Sudoku #5

				8		3	6	
				5	2		8	
3		8						2
			2			4		1
	9	3			8			
			9	4		6		
			5	3	9	7	1	4
	1							3
7					4			

Sudoku #6

	6	5		3	9		4	1
1							3	
				1				7
	7				5			
	3			9	6		7	
			2				9	
		6		4				
	8	7	1	5			6	4
	1					5		

Sudoku #7

9						2		6
			4					
					7			
				9	5	3		
		4				5		
	8							
5					9			
							8	
				2			4	7

Sudoku #8

	2					1	7	
1		7		6				9
3		8						
	9		4					
					2		6	
2	8		5		6	9	4	
						3		4
		4		5		6		7
	6						8	

Sudoku #1

			3				2	6
	1	8			5			
				6				3
	4					8	9	
	5			4				
2								
					4	5		
6								

Sudoku #2

	3				2			
	5							
						4		6
	2						3	
			8	6				7
		4						
			3			2	1	
6								
7			9					

Sudoku #3

				1				
		6					5	
				3	8			
1					2			
	8							
			5				9	7
		5				2		
		9	3					
				8				1

Sudoku #4

					6			
9		8						2
				1	4			7
			2				8	
	4							6
		5	3					
					7			
	1							
		3				9	5	

Sudoku #5

		6						
		3			5			
				8		7		
			6					3
7								
8				4				
9					1	8		
	4		3					5
							1	

Sudoku #6

					5			
					3		7	1
				8		2	5	4
	2			5	9		3	
8				7	6			
1								
							4	3
	8							6
4			6			1		2

Sudoku #7

5	1	8		4	3	7		
	9			8				2
							1	3
7			4					
	6		3	9	5			
					9			8
8		5						
	7			5		4	6	

Sudoku #8

	4			7		3		
						8		
				6				
		5						4
		8						
			1	4			6	
	3		8		9			
			5					
	1						7	

Sudoku #1

	3	4	7	1				8
	2	9			3			
		8				6	2	1
				3				
2					1		5	
	9		4		6	5	7	
5	8		3					

Sudoku #2

				1				
8								7
				3	9			
		9		4	1			
								5
	7					2		8
5			8					
	1						3	
							4	

Sudoku #3

				3		4		
						9		
	7	8						
4								
			7				8	2
							7	
				4	5			
	2						1	
3				6	9			

Sudoku #4

6								
2	9		5					
						8	7	
	6		2					9
		7			3	1		
				1	7			
					8			
	5							6

Sudoku #5

	4					5		
		1			6		8	
			3					
9								
						7		4
8		6			2			
			7					
		2					9	
			4	5				

Sudoku #6

9			4					
		2				6		
			5				8	
						3		
		6				2		1
	5		9					
				2				
	8						5	
		3		1				

Sudoku #7

		5		7	4	6		
					1			
2								9
				2				
						5	1	
8			3	9				
		6						
		4						
				8			7	3

Sudoku #8

				5			9	2
7		6						
1								8
4						7		
						3		
				8	2			
			7					
		2						6
			4			1		

Sudoku #1

							9	3
	6				5			
	5		7					
						7		2
9		4		8				
3								
	2				7	1		
8							4	
			6					

Sudoku #2

1		4						
								8
				3	5			7
					3			
4						9		
	5			8	7			
	7							
						6		
			9			4	1	

Sudoku #3

			5			4		
		2	8					
	3							6
								9
	6						7	3
5			1					
				3				
	9			7				
1						5		

Sudoku #4

		6					5	
				3				
1				2				
						2		
		8	7					
				4		3	1	
2								
			5		8			6
			6				7	

Sudoku #5

3					1			
					4			
		7						2
					3	1		
	8							
		2		8			5	
	5			2			6	
1						4		
				7				

Sudoku #6

	6					7		
		4			9			
						1	6	
	3				2			
	7							
					4			2
		2						9
	1		6					
		8		7				

Sudoku #7

2	4							
					1			5
	5	1						9
			2	7			6	
						7		
	6		3			2	4	
		3			9			

Sudoku #8

	3							
		2	7	9	3	5		
4	5							
8						2		
					4	3		
9					6	7		1
	7		2		5	1		
								6
					1			

Sudoku #1

		1				3	4	
6				7				
5	8	2			3	9		
	7	6	4		5	1		
		3	9	2			8	
			7		1	6	9	5
	6		8		2	4	1	9
4		5			7	2	3	8
8	2	9	3	1	4	5	7	6

Sudoku #2

5			1	2				
7	6			9	5			
4							5	
8	9	5	6			1		3
2	7	4	3		1	9		8
6		3	9				4	2
			8	6	7	3		
1	8	7		3	9	4	2	6
	5		2	1	4	8		7

Sudoku #3

	6			3	4			1
		1			2			
5	2			6			8	
3			2	9				8
7	5	9	6		8		2	
1			7	5			4	
	3	7	4		5	8	9	
8	1	4	3	2	9		6	7
	9	5		7	6	3	1	4

Sudoku #4

	7		4	8		6	2	
	3							9
1				6	5			
	5	4			9		1	
2	8	7	5	4	1		3	6
	9			3		5		2
7	6	9	2	1	4		8	
4		8	3		6	2	9	
5	2	3	7		8	1		

Sudoku #5

	4	7						
			3	9				
					1		8	6
5	6	1	4	7		9	2	
8		3						5
7		4	2	8				
1		5	9	6	8	2	3	
4		6	1	2	7	8		
9		2	5	3	4	7	6	1

Sudoku #6

	7		8		6			
	8		3					4
9	5					2		
7		2	1			6		
3		8	4		9		7	2
5	1	4	6					
8	4	7	9	6	3		2	
1	3	5					6	9
	2	9	5	4		8	3	7

Sudoku #7

	2				6	9	1	
							5	7
	4		1			8	3	
9			4	8		3	2	
8	3		6	1	2	5		
7	6		5	9				1
3		6	2	5	1	7	4	8
	7	1	3	6		2	9	5
		8	7	4	9			

Sudoku #8

		3			4			
					2	5		8
		9			8			
	1	7	2			4	3	6
							5	9
5	3		1	9	6	7	8	
8	4		6	2			7	1
	9		5	3	1	8		4
3	6	1		4	7	9	2	5

Sudoku #1

			8	5			4	
3		9						
1					6			3
	5							
			7				2	
	8						5	
					9			
6				1	3			

Sudoku #2

			3	6				
		7		9				
	2						5	
					1		4	
								3
		3				8		6
			8					9
5	4				2			
1								

Sudoku #3

	1		3		4	8		
						9		
	5	9	1					
				4				
1	2						9	
	8			2			7	4
	6	3		1				8
				7		6		
5	9				2	1		

Sudoku #4

					3		2	1
			9			4	6	7
					6			
	4		6		5		3	
		9	2		8			
		1						
							7	3
		7		8		1		4
	9							8

Sudoku #5

2	1		8			6		
						1		
6	9	3						5
4		6	1		8			
	3	5	2				9	
				8			5	
					3			
	6	2	7		1			

Sudoku #6

4	9				7			8
		3	6	4	8			2
	1			3		2		7
3	6	8						
1			2			5		
	8	5	1		3	6	2	

Sudoku #7

	5			6				
				2		4		9
		3					1	
				4				2
		1			8			
2					9			
6								
					1	3	8	

Sudoku #8

3		6						
			5	2				7
			7			8		
		1			9		6	
	7							
					3			
		8		1	6			
	5							2

Sudoku #1

8	4	5	3	9	1	2	6	7
7	6	1	8	5	2	3	4	9
3	2	9	6	7	4	8	1	5
1	7	4	9	2	6	5	8	3
2	5	6	1	3	8	7	9	4
9	3	8	7	4	5	1	2	6
4	8	3	2	6	7	9	5	1
5	1	7	4	8	9	6	3	2
6	9	2	5	1	3	4	7	8

Sudoku #2

8	5	4	3	6	7	2	9	1
3	1	7	2	9	5	6	8	4
9	2	6	1	4	8	3	5	7
6	8	5	7	3	1	9	4	2
2	9	1	4	8	6	5	7	3
4	7	3	5	2	9	8	1	6
7	3	2	8	5	4	1	6	9
5	4	9	6	1	2	7	3	8
1	6	8	9	7	3	4	2	5

Sudoku #3

7	1	2	3	9	4	8	6	5
4	3	8	2	5	6	9	1	7
6	5	9	1	8	7	4	3	2
3	7	6	9	4	5	2	8	1
1	2	4	7	3	8	5	9	6
9	8	5	6	2	1	3	7	4
2	6	3	4	1	9	7	5	8
8	4	1	5	7	3	6	2	9
5	9	7	8	6	2	1	4	3

Sudoku #4

4	7	6	8	5	3	9	2	1
5	8	3	9	2	1	4	6	7
9	1	2	4	7	6	3	8	5
2	4	8	6	1	5	7	3	9
7	3	9	2	4	8	5	1	6
6	5	1	7	3	9	8	4	2
8	2	5	1	9	4	6	7	3
3	6	7	5	8	2	1	9	4
1	9	4	3	6	7	2	5	8

How to play sudoku Fill in the empty fields with the numbers from 1 through 9 Every row must contain the numbers from 1 through 9 Every column must contain the numbers from 1 through 9 Every 3x3 square must contain the numbers from 1 through 9

www.ingramcontent.com/pod-product-compliance
Lightning Source LLC
Chambersburg PA
CBHW081417250726
48654CB00013B/1727
9798697933763